Violin Exam Pieces

ABRSM Grade 2

Selected from the 2012–2015 syllabus

Name

Date of exam

Contents

Violin consultant: Philippa Bunting
Footnotes: Edward Huws Jones (EHJ) and Anthony Burton

Other pieces for Grade 2

First published in 2011 by ABRSM (Publishing) Ltd, a wholly owned subsidiary of ABRSM, 24 Portland Place, London W1B 1LU, United Kingdom

© 2011 by The Associated Board of the Royal Schools of Music

Music origination by Andrew Jones
Cover by Økvik Design
Printed in England by Halstan & Co. Ltd, Amersham, Bucks.

March by Mr Handel

Edited by and continuo realized by
Philip Ledger

G. F. Handel

The German-born composer George Frideric Handel (1685–1759) spent the last 47 years of his life in England, becoming famous first for his operas and later for his oratorios – large-scale works for voices, chorus and orchestra on biblical or other moral subjects. The well-known chorus 'See, the conquering hero comes' was written in 1747 for one of these oratorios, *Joshua*, and later transferred into a revival of another, *Judas Maccabaeus*. This adaptation of its melody is the first item in a series called *Warlike Musick*, published in 1760 by John Walsh of London, and described as 'a Choice Collection of Marches & Trumpet Tunes for a German Flute, Violin or Harpsicord [sic], by Mr Handel, Sr Martini [Sammartini] and the most Eminent Masters'. The trills are editorial. The slurs and dynamics are suggestions for exam purposes and may be varied.

The Honeysuckle

A:2

Arranged by Edward Huws Jones

Antony Holborne

The Honeysuckle was published by Antony Holborne (*c*.?1545–1602) in 1599, during the last years of the reign of Elizabeth I, in an arrangement for five viols. It is also found in versions for lute and cittern (a wire-strung instrument rather like a flat-backed mandolin). The piece is a type of dance known as an almain, a lively and extrovert dance form with a two-in-a-bar feel, often played with a military swagger. Enjoy the bold crotchets which open each phrase in the first half. In the second half the dynamics (which are all editorial) can follow the delightful changes in the harmony. EHJ

A:3

French Troubadour Song

Edited by Gabriella Lenkei

Pál Járdányi

Pál Járdányi (1920–66) was a Hungarian composer, teacher, folk music specialist and writer on music. After beginning his studies as a violinist, he studied composition with Zoltán Kodály, and he followed in Kodály's footsteps as a collector and editor of traditional Hungarian songs. His compositions include many pieces for young performers. This *French Troubadour Song* is an imitation of the manner of the songs of the troubadours, poet-musicians of southern France in the 12th and 13th centuries. The drone of the hurdy-gurdy or *vielle* on which a troubadour might have accompanied himself is suggested by the left hand of the piano part and, at the end, by the use of the G string.

Heidenröslein

D. 257

B:1

Arranged by ABRSM

Franz Schubert

Heidenröslein Little Briar-Rose

The Austrian composer Franz Schubert (1797–1828) wrote operas, symphonies and a great deal of instrumental music, but he is chiefly famous for his songs for voice and piano – more than 600 of them, including some of the greatest ever written. This is an arrangement of 'Heidenröslein', one of five songs he wrote on a single day, 19 August 1815, to words by the great poet Johann Wolfgang von Goethe. Its folk-like melody matches the folk-like poem, about a boy who plucks a wild rose despite its threats to defend itself with its thorns.

B:2

Theme from *William Tell*

Arranged by Mary Cohen

Gioachino Rossini

Gioachino Rossini (1792–1868) was a famous composer of operas, most of them for theatres in his native Italy, but the last four for the Opéra in Paris, the city where he then settled into a long retirement. His very last opera, first performed in 1829, was *Guillaume Tell*, a stirring story about the legendary 14th-century hero William Tell, whose resistance to Austrian rule is said to have led to the founding of the Swiss nation. The overture which precedes the opera has a closing section with this famous melody in the quick dance time of the galop. It became even better known when it was used in *The Lone Ranger*, a popular television Western series of the 1950s.

Londonderry Air

B:3

Arranged by Edward Huws Jones

Trad. Irish

One of the best-known Irish slow airs, *Londonderry Air* first appeared in print in the mid-19th century. The story goes that the melody was collected by one Jane Ross of the County of Londonderry, from the playing of a blind fiddler. Since then, various lyrics have been set to the tune, perhaps most famously 'Danny Boy' by Frederic Weatherly. The eloquent and expansive melody invites the violinist to enjoy the lyrical qualities of the instrument. Above all, the player needs to keep something in reserve for bar 13, where the melody reaches its peak. EHJ

DO NOT PHOTOCOPY
© MUSIC

Sher

Arranged by Coen Wolfgram

Abe Schwartz

This is an example of klezmer, a style of folk music for groups of instruments, typically played at weddings, which originated in the Jewish communities of central and eastern Europe in the 19th century, and was spread throughout the world when many of the musicians were forced to emigrate. One such emigrant was Abe Schwartz (1881–1963), who was born in Romania but moved to the United States in 1899 and established himself there as a composer, violinist, pianist and bandleader. He is credited as the composer of *Sher*, an example of a group dance requiring quick movements of the legs, named after the shears (in Yiddish 'scher') of tailors. **In the exam the repeat must be played**; students may like to vary the dynamic the second time.

School Break

No. 6 from *24 Easy Little Concert Pieces*

C:2

István Szelényi

István Szelényi (1904–72) was a Hungarian composer, pianist and teacher, also known for his editions of piano music by Liszt. A composition student of Zoltán Kodály, he wrote several large-scale oratorios for chorus and orchestra, concertos and other orchestral music, and a good deal of chamber music. His set of *24 Easy Little Concert Pieces*, published in 1958, includes this miniature built on harmonies of 4ths and, at the end, 5ths. The composer has indicated tenutos in the first phrase; players may like to use them in the following phrases as well.

Mango Walk

Arranged by Sheila Nelson

Trad. Jamaican

'Mango Walk' is a traditional children's song from the Caribbean island of Jamaica, about stealing fruit from an orchard. In 1938 the Australian-born composer Arthur Benjamin adapted it as the theme of his *Jamaican Rumba* for two pianos (and later orchestra). This version by Sheila Nelson, well known for her many collections of string teaching pieces and for her history *The Violin and Viola*, is also in the dance rhythm of the rumba.